Molly Naylor is a poet, scriptwriter, performer and filmmaker. She is the co-writer and creator of Sky One sitcom *After Hours*. She has been commissioned by organisations including BBC Radio 4, Sky, the BFI, the Royal Shakespeare Company, Creative England, the Bush Theatre, Oxford Playhouse and Battersea Arts Centre. She has written and starred in three live shows, *Whenever I Get Blown Up I Think of You*, *My Robot Heart* and *If Destroyed Still True*. She has performed at festivals and events all over the world. Her essays and poems have been published in the *Rialto*, the *North*, *Under the Radar*, *Grazia* and the *Independent*. She is the host and co-creator of True Stories Live. This is her first collection.

www.mollynaylor.com

GW00455478

Badminton

Molly Naylor

Burning Eye

BurningEyeBooks
Never Knowingly
Mainstream

This edition published by Burning Eye Books 2016

www.burningeye.co.uk
@burningeyebooks

Burning Eye Books
15 West Hill, Portishead, BS20 6LG

ISBN 978-1-909136-87-8

Molly Naylor gratefully ackowledges support from Arts Council England in writing this book:

LOTTERY FUNDED

Supported using public funding by
ARTS COUNCIL
ENGLAND

For Jack

Badminton can be read in any order, but the best way to read it is from start to finish. Part one, 'Beginnings', consists of poems that are young, hopeful or speak directly to the start of things. Part two, 'Middles', is sticky. The poems here try to unpick feelings, events and encounters. Part three, 'Endings', is about doomed love, failure and acceptance. It's about learning and letting go. The book as a whole attempts to address our human predicament in a way that is silly, open-hearted and unapologetic. These poems have been written quickly, fought with and then abandoned. They asked to be written, mostly at inopportune times – on trains, in fields, in bars and in the backs of taxis. I made this book for the same reason that I make all my work – ultimately, because it makes me feel better. I hope that you find something useful in here too.

'We had absolutely horrible, horrible equipment, which is one reason I think it sounded so good.'

Maureen 'Moe' Tucker

CONTENTS

BEGINNINGS

MIDDLES

ENDINGS

BEGINNINGS

HELLO

I haven't tried this in a while.
I don't know what it was.
The snarky academics, perhaps,
or the heartache, or the spirituality
or the availability of so many
different types of food.

Perhaps it was because of
all the films I hadn't seen.
All the Al Pacinos
lit by unreal street lamps,
fake rain making meaning
in swift, effective chemical reactions,
my heart breaking easily
frame after frame.

I suppose I'm looking to try again.
Get back into it.
Why not try submitting a shopping list
to an experimental anthology,
a literary friend suggests –
or describing trees or something?

I've been playing a lot of badminton.
I like talking about badminton.
I like badminton.
It's everything that this isn't.
When you have doubts
you can just aim for the face.

Plus, I got tired of words;
that's really it.
They're such a tiny part
of how we speak.

FOR THE FLUSHING FERRY

She took us to school.
She was strong in a storm.

My fingers tapped secrets
into her seats
and the leap between
her and the shore
taught my legs to
run without falling.
They were strong
and they won all the races.

On choppy days
our stomachs lurched and sank
and it was as if she was telling us:
you need to think about death more.

We were kids, so
maybe she was right.
We were Drumstick lollies
and paper aeroplanes;
we were packed lunch,
mocking and spots;
we were midnight feasts
and knee-scabs
and we were stirred
by the things underneath us.

The day the fishermen caught
a shark and showed us
was better than Easter,
better than Christmas.

These days I look at octopuses
on the Internet.
Last year I had a freak-out
and almost bought a barge on eBay.
I submerge myself in water
at every opportunity

and I probably need to
think about death more.

Recently, on a rare visit
back to the coast
I spied her across the harbour,
soaring past smugglers' caves and
yachts with names like 'Triumph',
and that night I dreamt of running,
my legs as strong as waves.

ASK

This morning is too predictable.
Like yesterday, and the day before,
I wake up thinking about you.
So I go downstairs, eat muesli
to prove that I'm not a failure,
and I find something to
twat myself over the head with.
I'm still thinking about you,
only now I have a headache too.

So I will find solace
in a real-time road movie,
swap pining for driving
and get out of here.
Liking someone who doesn't have a clue
belongs to cringing teenagers,
like drinking cider on beaches,
like thinking Green Day are good.

The problem with driving is this:
the road reminds me of you.
The lampposts are you bent over.
The tall woman at the drive-through
is you in Toyota-blue eyeshadow.

After slow miles of chevron-yous
I stop in a Little Chef,
order the Olympic Breakfast
and congratulate myself –
I have not thought of you
in whole moments.
I look down. Oh.
I have made you out of my fry-up.

Back on the road and the sky is not you
but the clouds are the kind you'd paint
if you painted,
on the radio the presenter is you

doing an impression of a dickhead,
a bleak pig farm on the left
is totally you.

Thinking of you gets me
nowhere but here,
a dual carriageway
on a nothing afternoon;
you are also, somehow
the promise in the distance,
a sunset, no, a service station,
a horizon with illusion
keeps my foot on the pedal,
keeps me singing along to you.
You are the shipping forecast
and the traffic news.

This car is due for its MOT
and everyone we know
is slowly falling apart.
Far from teenagers and
it's not okay to send you a note
via my mate, to your mate:
Will you go out with me?
Tick yes, cross no.

If I asked you now
I'd be ridiculous.
A grown woman on a skateboard,
proffering a cake
iced like a bloody heart.

But. Teenagers know everything.
And growing older is shedding that.
I sometimes miss the magic of
cider-courage and Tippex declarations,
of being earnest and immortal
while the sun rises over Truro.

Maybe I should drive to your house.
Maybe you'd smell of
Lambert & Butler and Lynx Africa
and chips and Tippex
and *Goldeneye* and
'Everybody Hurts' by REM.

The problem with adulthood
is that it doesn't have a smell.
Bacon eyebrows suit you
and the rain against the headlights
made my heart swell.

ROOFTOPS

Our children will go shoeless as
we've spent our money on breakfasts,
your flat is in the attic and
you only have a mattress,
the moon looks through the skylight
at a room with no design,
bluebells drooping in a pint glass
as temporary as a frown.

SOMEONE ELSE'S FAMILY

The party was in a garden
in late September, Kentish Town.
It was trying to still be summer
so we tried not to be cold.

Somebody's niece gave me
a cloak and made me play.
We took off our shoes
and I handed her my hat.
She coated it in leaves
and said it was a crown.
What would you do
if you were queen?
I asked, shivering,
pretending to be warm.

She shrugged and later
fell asleep across my legs
beside a fire somebody's dad had built.

ALL THIS TALKING IN PUBLIC PLACES

Some days I miss waitressing
and the way it made my feet feel.
And not just waitressing:
scrubbing things,
stacking things
and dancing on tables.

The attention to hair removal,
making your mascara black as spiders,
dressing like the idea of a girl.

There's a simplicity
in belonging to people
who think you're not all that.

On getting home
you find your head's got songs in it
and your jokes are still intact
as you pile your bones into a bathtub
and watch yourself becoming clean.

TARANTINO

I only came to see this film tonight
so I could feel closer to America.

All my life I've been waiting to be found.
Then one spring day I let that go.
Decided I should sell my things and head there,
America! So stupid and so desolate,
all expanse and milkshakes
and everything geared up
to help you lose yourself.
Lost was my new found;
that became my shiny plan.

But tonight in the back of the cinema,
I have the thought that
I might be lying.
It might be a cover-up
for a secret fantasy
that America will see and
fall in love with me,
in some wild and distant way,
will name a burger after me
and I will be found after all,
my character honed and snappy,
like the dialogue in this film.
So much of it disguised as superfluous
but every bit of chaos essential and whole.

THE IMMORTALITY PROJECT
Or 'Poem Not to Read Out at a Wedding'

You are in a department store
agonising over a present
for a friend's wedding,
a marriage that won't just be a marriage
but an immortality project.
You will raise your fizzy wine
to a future that looks, in direct sunlight,
like an embroidered cushion
depicting an old woman
cradling a miniature dog
in the manner of someone
who doesn't believe that
her grandchildren will have funerals.

The wedding will take place
in the community centre
of your shared childhoods
where Scout leaders aimed
to keep you forever alive
with church squash and Rich Tea.

After the disco there will be
a paternal heart-to-heart
which won't just be a heart-to-heart
but an attempt at receiving
a massive forgiveness
to deflect unanswered questions
from hospital-bed ghosts.

At the end of the party
the happy couple will depart.
Her heart, his heart, off
to wrestle out the listlessness,
repress all that they'll miss
and make preemptive soothing stories
from the weak handshakes
and infidelities
of their unborn sons.

ARMOUR

There are knights in shining armour
but there are also clowns.
Clumsy people whose feet
feel ten feet long,
whose hot hands hang
as cumbersome as oven gloves.

Who wish they were
as sexy as Brazilians,
who feel most comfortable on moors,
the ones who spend parties
crouching with children
and never know what to do
with their face.

For whom pride is a friend
you keep meaning to phone,
who don't know what
they're scrolling down for,
who are not strangers to beetroot faces,
who get by on pretending,
who never eat without spilling
and laugh wide with wonky teeth.

Those who sleep on trains
with their bags on the seat,
whose memories contain
no chainmail victories
or horseback-noble dignities
but cringe-images of smashing plates,
squeaky shoes at funerals
and classroom presentations
with prune-bruises covering both knees.

Those who, on cycling home through town
from a thing that made them itchy,
might skid to a stop
at the sight of true magic –

a penguin tap-dancing
or a puddle with a face –
then curse their hope and realise
that it was just a plastic bag
before riding off again faster,
half-drunk and mumbling
you clown, you clown,
you clown.

Those who may not know that
it's okay to not be a knight,
that more sightly than a suit of armour
is a custard pie to the face.
Awkwardness in place of grace.
A fool, who doesn't know how to battle
and doesn't clink and shimmer
when they walk.

SELF-PORTRAIT AT THIRTY-TWO ON A TRAIN OUTSIDE CHELMSFORD

I might be old enough for a dog.
Not a big one – a normal one.
I have two brothers.
I like my friends.
I make quick decisions;
it's how I survive.
I own four nice cups.
I know how to drive.

I'm trying to learn history.
I've been getting up earlier.
It's embarrassingly hard.
I'm trying to see life
as bright and bracing,
a car boot sale at dawn
full of promise and bad coffee
and other people's junk.

I'm learning how to make meals
that are basic but tasty.
I want to do a recipe book called
Heartbreak Food for Humans with Weird Faces.

I saw a kid on the beach last week,
holding up an object and shouting, *Dad,*
look at this! I love this, what is this?
She was standing in the shallows
and the waves just kept coming.

I'm aiming to be ambitious.
But always appropriate, too.
I'm trying to be 'always' too.
To always be always.

Every day I put something down
and pick something else up.
I worry that I'm trading in the wrong things.

Swapping the memory of the
warm-damp-grass-start-of-the-holidays feeling
for knowing the capital of Georgia
or having a handle on death.

No two snowflakes are alike
but I bet some are fucking similar
and I give myself four more non-settling years,
asking drunk in the mirror sometimes –
But is that a gift?

I'm trying out this new thing: it's
seeing things just as they are.
I owe it to the teenage me
in the cut-up clothing who thought
that anywhere was better than now.

Sometimes I think all life is
is wandering around,
eating different things,
trying not to be mean.
On better days I think –
look at life! I love life, what is life?

The train's pulling in now.
I'm meeting some friends in a café
where the floor is made of maps.
Every minute I get closer
to reaching them.

Some of them have dogs.
Some of them can drive.
I like my friends.
I hope they survive.

And then there's everybody else, outside,
their decisions bumping into each other,
moving them through space
in a city that's also a heart.
At least, that's how
I picture it looking
from above.

MIDDLES

EARLHAM CEMETERY NOVEMBER

Knock-off iPod in my pocket,
I jog among the sadly missed.
It's not just autumn leaves that glow
but the best-kept graves I've ever seen.

Tattoos aren't really permanent,
sand was once proud rock,
everything you've said is gone
and that dusty smell in books is rot.

I fell for a drowning man once.
Watched him walk to the sea from the shore.
As his outstretched hand slipped under,
I'd never loved him more.

ADMINISTRATIVE ROMANTIC PICNIC

After a telly meeting
with yet another woman called Jess
I find a tiny patch of
not yet dead grass in Soho,
barely reached by puny April sunshine,
and think of all the things I could have said.
Jess had removed her eyebrows
and drawn on some other eyebrows.
I think she would have bullied me in school.

A man and woman sit down nearby.
The man gets out a blanket
plus plates, cutlery, a big salad.
They eat fast, knees not quite touching,
then go back to work.
Their lunch is no-fuss,
well-rehearsed, nutritious.
Designed to keep them
both alive for longer.

I think of all the things I could have done.
I could have made a big salad
instead of downing the croissant
that Jess offered me with words
but not with eyebrows.

I could have stayed with that boy
from sixth form
who my family liked
and who in this thin sunlight
might have tried to make me
live for ages too.

DINOSAUR

I am drinking coffee at an airport Costa
with an adorable eighty-year-old xenophobe.
He's not racist, but.
Dinosaur, I think, and smile, and sip.

The dinosaur doesn't think much of millennials.
I am watching him watching them walk by,
career-identities tattooed down their sleeves:
juice enthusiast, yoga dude, Frisbee interventionist,
urban life-coach, PhD in surfing, beard personality definer,
worrier that friends are too white.

Drinking coffee with the dinosaur is the opposite of
the blind faith coffee shop near my flat
where they give you your liberal checklist
to tick while you sip –
this sounds like the kind of thing I think.
This must be proof that I exist.

I don't know why I let him buy me coffee
but I did, so here we are.

After a while I start tuning him out,
in case he dies while I'm with him
or in case he says something
that I agree with.

BOWLING

The first time I went bowling
I didn't want to give up my shoes.
How will anyone know who I am?
I asked the shoe guy.
Or who anyone else is?
How will I work out who in the bowling alley
I want to have sex with?
He didn't answer.
He just spritzed my trainers
with antibacterial spray
and handed me my size four brogues.

It's hard to get really good at bowling.
I'm saying this so as
not to offend bowling experts.
The truth is, bowling is easy.
You can make a strike on your first ever go.
Rolling the ball round to find the holes,
you immediately look like a pro.

The lanes alternate between
high-fiving amateurs
and stoical teams of experts
in customised black and pink jackets
who don't smile when they win
and are elegantly non-ironic.

When we bowl
we are in a film.
That's why I like to bowl –
for the precision of fantasy
and the dress-up anonymity
that comes with handing over
those strapless mules which scream:
I'm strong but ultimately lonely
or those gold pumps which shout:
I didn't get into drama school.

One night the bowling alley
I go to burned down.
Nobody was hurt
but the slushy machine melted
and we weren't allowed back in
to get our shoes.

It was hard to say goodbye
to the other bowlers
even though we hadn't
spoken before the fire,
even though I didn't know them
because their feet were so neutral.
I loved them
because we could've died,
and because I didn't hate them yet.
Their shoes hadn't given them away.

A SINNER'S GUIDE TO MINDLESSNESS

Centre yourself.
Check with the Internet
that your haircut's okay.
Suppress any suspicion
that we are made of grains
and you can build music with science.

Text late-night desperate missives
to joyless blood relatives –
I am not just physics.
I am the greatest story ever told;
look how many people watch me.

Centre yourself.
Make a list of what you deserve.
Type a nightclub toilet reminder
that dancing's more than just
riffing on the heartbeat.
Hungover, swap exercise for
echo-chamber high-fives
and sleep through the news.

Take a moment to meditate
on times you were wronged during
kiss-chase and hide-and-seek.
Replace the fluorescent stars on your ceiling
with a montage of your GCSE set texts.

Tell children there's no way that aliens exist
because surely if they did
they'd be dying to meet us,
particularly you, with your lovely haircut
which has found its way through algorithms
to the people who will tell you it's perfect.

RUPERT MURDOCH'S EASTER

Rupert isn't entirely certain why
he organises the Easter egg hunt
at his mansion every year.
On a calm, overcast day
he'll look out from his veranda,
the grey shapes of the biggest trees
like battleships on the distant hills,
and he's sure that he's doing it
out of a gentle, bumbling benevolence
befitting a man of his years.
No, Dad, he says to his acres.
This isn't cynical;
this is a real Easter egg hunt,
not a preemptive deathbed regret deterrent,
thank you very much, Dad.

Rupert's dad would never
have made an Easter egg hunt
for his grandchildren
although to be entirely fair
he was probably too busy
doing the war.

No, on a good day Rupert knows
he's doing it for the kids.
The smallest grandchildren
and their pissy friends
who only really laugh
when someone falls over.

The oldest grandchild, Nina, won't join in.
She's fifteen, unattractive, idealistic,
says things to him like,
Rummaged through Vanessa Feltz's bins lately, have you?
Well, fuck Nina and her badges
and her principles
and the nose ring
that isn't even a nose ring.

She knows nothing of real rebellion.
He knows mutiny like a dying aunt,
he's lived with it.

No, it's the snotty ones he does it for
and he's chuckling now
as he shuffles under hedges
thinking of their faces.
He's making it harder than ever this year
so that the day lasts longer.
Three hundred golden eggs
made by a chocolate mogul in Bern.

Last year, they found all fifty
in under an hour and then left.
A flurry of buggies and
sticky hugs and glitter and
he had to spend
the late afternoon trapped
inside the shapes they left behind.
A cigar and a good Grappa
and an ugly sunset.
The house became
a decommissioned cruise-liner.
People leaving is worse
than them not having arrived.
He was hoovering up glitter for days.

No, he's going to get so much food in
for the grown-ups that
they won't *want* to leave.
Gluten and gluten-free and no excuses;
he just doesn't want them
to go before it's dark.
If it's still light when they leave
he'll get stuck in the twilight
brain-scroll down to the comments section
or remember the way his father used to look at him

all epic and odd like a sunfish.
It's hard to justify yourself
to fathers and live animals.
This is why Rupert likes to hunt.
So he can shoot them in their faces
and be proud of his empire.

He wedges the last egg
up the drainpipe,
rubs his lower back
and nods himself satisfied.
Maybe this year they'll stay for ages
because he's not all-over ghastly
and everyone likes finding
something golden.

LITTLE CHEF

When I used to waitress
I would moan like crazy.
At twenty-one I couldn't bear the
petty tyrannical cutlery stuff.
We're talking up-market places too,
not Wimpy bars or Little Chefs –
I was horrible at suffering.

The A17 is a road made of
clouds and crisp packets
and there's this diner
I sometimes stop at
miles away from houses.

This kid works there who'll make
your tea with such precision and care.
He'll smile while fielding orders from
a relentless asshole boss,
all power-trip invented jobs –
after that you're washing under the bins,
after that you're scouring the oven shelves,
after that you're telling my wife
about my affair with Keith
and no, you can't have a cigarette break,
you might use it to plan your escape.

I offered to turn my hired Ford Escort
into a getaway car once
and he laughed and said
it's really not that bad
compared to all the things
he signs petitions for online
so I drove off without him.

I wanted to tell you about him
in case you were ever driving by
or in case you wanted
to take the trip especially,
make a day of seeing someone
being beautiful at suffering.

42

HOW TO KILL YOUR PLANTS

At an early age, it's important to develop
an unhealthy relationship
with dance shoes and attention.

Teenage, tell your mother
you don't want to end up like her,
send lavish presents later
to prove that you were right.

In your twenties, squint your way through broadsheets
unpicking the puzzling stitches of suburbia.
In the supermarket, pick up
peace lilies and rubber plants as
afterthoughts under strip-lights,
a trolley canopy above your solo shopping.

When you're thirty, immerse yourself
in water at every opportunity.
Tell yourself you know music
and roam around Brixton.
Don't think of Clare Anderson
from sixth form with her babies.

Let your once-green shoots
droop lonesome all winter,
then, in the last week before spring,
drown them.
An oops minute of care
after a year of neglect.
Then walk away and know
that some people
just aren't meant to grow things.

2016 RULES OK

In a departure lounge
I scroll through
non-news stories:
PERSON MARRIES PERSON
BUZZARD IS AMAZING
CRISPS REMAIN DELICIOUS.

I imagine flushing my phone
down the aeroplane toilet,
my contacts spilling into the Alps,
so that my holiday isn't spent
assembling the lives of my enemies
through their small successes
or fake-lamenting
my friends' airbrushed crises
or reading a liberal broadsheet's feature
on moving to the wilderness.

I put it in my pocket instead because
no age thinks it's a wonderful age,
especially not one with so much
personalised global suffering
at its thumb-tips.

And we do fly now
and cure people
and remember the time
you raised all that money
by fast-walking 5k
and telling online that you ran?

And we've made rockets
and phone masts which
are made of cells like bodies
and loom over fields,
fierce with our pictures.

There's one in the hills
above the town where I grew up.

I like to imagine it in analogue,
lonely in the wide darkness of a field,
manned by one woman,
all our text messages
keeping her up.
She can't clock off
until we are all asleep.
Her palms yawn around a Thermos flask
as she sends us to each other.

THINGS SAID TO ME IN MEETINGS WITH TELEVISION EXECUTIVES

Can you just change the gays a bit?
Hugo has never met gays like these.
Trouble is, there just aren't any black directors.
I like your shoes, are they from the nineties?
Norwich... is that in Cornwall?

We're not really doing subtle this year,
we did too much subtle last year.
Do people actually work in fruit and veg shops, though?
I need you to make this 35% funnier.
Can you use your Oyster card in Norwich?

As a working class guy from Walton-on-the-Naze,
I really relate to this character's struggle.
Not that my parents were unemployed
and I mean our house was pretty big
but that was only because my gran died.

Gay is so hot this year
bi is so hot this year
trans is so hot this year
refugees are so right now
whereabouts in London is Norwich?

Thing is, men don't watch female shows.
Women watch male shows
because there aren't many female shows.
What's more millennial, a high-five or a fist-bump?
Listen, I just don't feel that she's a lesbian.

It's *Girls*, but with boys,
it's *Jurassic Park* meets *Brookside*,
it's *The Apprentice* meets *Five Children and It*,
it's *Jaws*, but if Jaws was a man and the sea was all women.
Norwich? Is that where that guy is from?

Hugo's still not convinced by the gays...

what if one of them was a tap-dancer?
Can we make her mixed-race as a compromise?
People won't watch it if she's in a wheelchair.

You said you didn't want a coffee, didn't you?
Keep sending us stuff, won't you?
Back to Norwich, then, is it?
Where did you say that was?

PYLONS

We had the most romantic day, didn't we?
The sun was low in the sky,
the forest was sandy and soft,
the branches made frames
for the red sky behind
and these knockout scenes
in no way passed me by.
But still, I felt a tug for pylons.
Motels. Motorways. Stationery.
Something that would last a little longer.

I don't want to bump into you in years
in a last-night-on-earth diner
and say, over a shared milkshake,
Oh, remember forests and
the sun hanging low in the sky
and the time we believed in something
for thirty minutes?
Old cowboys dipping curly fries into ketchup
a greasy apocalypse aphrodisiac
that would be killing us
if we weren't already doomed.

I want to get over beginnings
and get under a body that looks like a body
not a silhouette of a movie body
and work on getting used to things.
Like the sound of seagulls in the morning,
like living underneath a flightpath.

I want to kiss beside a sewage works.
Hold hands under pylons.

I'm not saying I wasn't breathless.
I still carry a bit of forest in my pocket,
and remember that fucking sunset?
It's just that it was easier
to be lovers there than not.

It's harder to love pylons than trees,
but that shouldn't stop us trying.
Think of them.
They are the looming guards of fields, fierce with ugly
function;
they are essential, intricate and normal
and there is a way
to find them gorgeous.

DRIVE

The night is darkest across the fens.
I'm looking out for badgers and deer,
afraid of shadows darting road-bound
towards the light only I am making.

I complain about the driving
but it's the best bit:
the gut-wrench playlists
that make crying a thing,
the crying that makes
knee-driving roll-ups more legal,
the smoking that hides the rising suspicion
I've been a dick.

There is communication I should respond to,
a person I am supposed to fall in love with,
but I keep driving under star blankets,
switch to full-beam and just keep driving.

ENDINGS

THERE IS THIS MAN, THIS MOMENT

I have sexy, difficult shoes on and
I am feeling clever and episodic,
the kind of mood I get into
at the weddings of vague friends
where I can regale dads anonymously
and no one really cares if I leave.

I can't stop thinking about death now
but not in a bad way.
Just – quick, help me do my bidding,
which is anything I want it to be –
drinking or sex or stories
or raising children,
I'm not that bothered anymore.
I've even started to find
my old school discos funny
and I no longer ache when I see
an old man on a bench
unwrapping sandwiches carefully.

This is a boot in the face of
bottomless, clutchy longing,
the type that made me profess my love
to a thin, mean hockey player
in a Radisson Blu hotel bar
because I didn't know how to not.

Today, there is just this moment,
this man who smells of old wood
who shows me pictures
of his children
and barely pretends
not to have that wife.

We kiss and then depart.
As I back onto my train
I see fragments of – ha! – love
in his eyebrows

so I love him right back – snap –
to see how it feels right then.
I pull the train door shut,
find an empty double seat
and I'm rocked to sleep
by more moments
carrying me forward,
carrying me on.

ANOTHER GOOD WOMAN LOST

When my friend Elizabeth finally met the man of her dreams,
she wanted to tell me all about him.
Lots of fun facts, like
how the man of her dreams
wakes up early, then
snoozes through the hours
he said he'd do volunteer work in.
The man of her dreams' granny
bought him a PlayStation
to thank him for looking after her
and because he can't afford his own.
On Mondays he makes his granny lunch –
crumpets, a Petit Filou –
then heads into her living room
to shoot computerised woman cops.

She told me how he's mysterious.
Like, at parties, he could be on the roof
thumb-swiping through
old dick pics in his sent box.

The man of her dreams owns a laptop
so future-thin that the screen
can't support its own weight and
on trains he emails from the vestibule
with it gaffer-taped to an easel.

When I met the man of her dreams
he bought me a half-pint
of Cornish Pilsner
in a bar that was basically a cave.
He listed his subtleties –
the *Blue Peter* badge he almost won,
his cousin with MS who he hates,
the time he pushed Michael Starling
out of a dinghy at Residential.
He asked me if I'd ever thought
about joining a gym.

I met her for coffee last week and
asked her how it was going.
She was so thirsty and hungover,
speaking desolately about seeing vitamins
in his *Star Wars* wash-bag,
her heart gasping at the sweet, private ways
in which he takes care of himself.

She couldn't stay long.
The man of her dreams
wanted her to meet his family
so she had cancelled her art class
to get the train to Bracknell.

I watched her walk towards the tube
and saw a man carrying a dachshund
shoulder-barge her, hard.
I watched her face fold into an apology
before he'd even looked at her,
before she'd felt the pain.

ESTATE AGENT

This is the house.
It has everything you asked for.
The hallway smells of
cinema seats and cinnamon
just like we discussed.

If you look from across the street
you can see the fairy lights
strung across the mantelpiece
like in the plan we made at Wetherspoons
all those months ago.
I hope you haven't changed.

If you walk to the end of the road
you'll still make out the privet hedge,
domes and peacocks I cut with scissors.
It was no big deal.
I still have blisters.

If you step back further still,
then even further
until you're at the place
where sky becomes space,
you can just see
your home's outline
and beside it the man
who's also yours
stood rigid, he's your rock,
your iron pole.

I'll leave you now, to settle in.
Make some memories
that will last as long as skin.

THE WRECKING SEASON

Listen to the whispers of the washed-up,
the weathered, the storm-brought.
Touch the shapes of things
moved by time and tide.
Fall for their foreign stories.

Contained in the washed-up
is the wisdom of cliffs and the
history of all those turquoise decades.
Think of it – we never thought we'd end up here.
No one ever does.

And we can never go back.
Broken bottles reunited would find
their smoothed edges unable
to tessellate with their missing parts even
if miracles brought them together.
Days, like waves, just keep on coming.

Battered and brave in bays, on beaches,
we tell our stories to sailors and dogs,
ignored by joggers and holidaymakers but
treasured by souls who appreciate things
that are worn or weathered, forgotten or odd.

LARKING

Remember that time a few years back
when your dad hadn't died
and we didn't think about
cancer so much?

When you were selling windows
and I was supporting a woman
with learning difficulties,
and thinking all day about treats.

I had less kindness about me
but being mean was funnier then.

It's not like we didn't know
about cancer or divorces;
we just hadn't factored in
the admin of sadness.
The way life isn't ever
what you deserve
and that deserving
is something we invented,
like bunting, like boxsets,
our need to commemorate
then forget.

These days there isn't even time to pray
and, God, we miss it now.
The singularity of wanting.
The quiet of our selfish needs.

IT'S A LOVELY DAY FOR BLAME

We can't figure out where we went wrong.
So we've decided to blame the Mayans.
Those pesky Mayans and the end of everything.
Perhaps it wasn't the Mayans, though.
Perhaps it was the chairs.
Perhaps if we'd sat on beanbags for long enough,
thought lightbulbs would have zinged us
from stupid to winning.

Chairs are just chairs,
let's not blame the chairs.
Let's blame Hitler.
Too obvious.
Let's blame Jackson Pollock,
the splatterers and the
you-can't-know-what-this-means gang
and all the fucking Damiens.
Let's blame the cousins with Christian hair,
the secretaries who wear it like a lanyard,
let's blame Rachel, Ross, Hugh Grant,
Walt Disney, all nostalgic narrative
and never watch films again.

What about your father's voice
or my mother's hands,
like mine but bigger,
like yours but shriller?
Let's blame the conventional clothes of this time,
the Relentless drinks and the numbers in the food.
Let's blame the fact that
I never threw my knickers at you
and you don't come from Wales.
Let's blame the Queen
for not knowing us, or
we could blame my PE teacher
for being impossibly mean
and the things from History class
that wouldn't go in.

Let's blame the sunrise smoking sessions
and the all-duvet mornings
we planned to make post-jogging,
pancake-flipping success stories.
Let's blame your sister
because her wedding was boring
and that was the reason
I puked on my feet.

Let's blame books.
I think it was books,
the column by your bed,
the way it wobbled and shook
as I added to it every Christmas.
But books are good,
everybody thinks so,
let's blame something colder.
Let's blame the snow and
the things I saw in its melt –
the dogshit Slush Puppie
and the dead wagtail.
Let's blame the hospital smell
that wouldn't wash off
and the cloud-tinged supermarket dash
when we were too hungry
to not just buy crisps and eggs.
Let's blame Austria.
Let's blame all jazz.
Let's blame my ex-boyfriend's boxers,
still under my bed.

What about we blame satellites?
Sky. The lost telescope instructions.
The meteor shower that never came.

What if we blame
your side-effects
and my bad back that
kept us in bed ignoring the knocks

or our battered bodies and
the way they looked
stretched across sofas?
Although if we do
we're getting closer
and we should probably
just stop.

OBITUARY OF A FAILED RELATIONSHIP

When it ended
they couldn't figure out
whose fault it was
so they decided not to blame anyone.
Especially not Hitler
or any furniture.

They had good taste in furniture.
She once mended a beanbag he split
by jumping on it from a great height.

They understood some modern art –
they were tolerant
and never said things like
A child could do that.

They made sandwiches for a funeral once
and they worked well together,
a witty conveyor belt
under village hall strip-light.

People say she sometimes looked at him
as if she wanted
to throw her knickers at him.
It is possible that he might
have had Welsh ancestry.

They didn't make pancakes very often,
but when they did they were
industrious and streamlined,
no first-go flop sacrifice to the ceiling or bin.
They sometimes gave up on books
but they read out loud
and were most of the time warm.

They were going to go to Vienna,
they were going to learn the constellations,
they were going to start doing yoga.

They looked after each other
until they couldn't.
But until they couldn't
they could.
And they did.

I DON'T KNOW WHY YOU INVITED JARED ANYWAY

Did I ever tell you
about that time
I drunk-drove to
Winterton-on-Sea in heavy fog
with a man who
could lie in his sleep?
Probably not.
It's not a dinner-party-type story.

If I told it at a dinner party
I would a bit ruin the night.
I'd have to *be* the dinner party
gesticulating wildly,
and then, and then, and then...

That guy Jared from your work
who doesn't know anyone
would find me inappropriate
but I think I could make it entertaining.

As a story it has everything.
A car chase.
A love interest.
A plot twist, some weather,
and there's a happy ending.
I present: my personality!

The moral message
might be slightly confusing
but only to Jared, that *wanker*.
My friends would see it
in the very act of
me happily eating olives
with this bunch of bastards
and now finding love
in predictable places
like living rooms and coffee shops

instead of car rides that feel
like suicide pacts.

And if I told the story once
I'd never have to tell it again.
In fact, even today
the details seem hazy
because I only think about it
now and then.

THIS IS THE RIVER

This is the river.
The one that transports the broken,
the tourist, the drunk
the holidaymakers eyeballing kingfishers
and the reborn,
their old chocolate-salesman selves
drowned far upstream from here.

This is the river
and I have been drifting.
Waiting for something
to hold me still.

This is the river
and it isn't Los Angeles
but it tempers the selfish
and carries the sick.

I have swum in many rivers
and I have so many rivers in me,
miles of them,
those blue roads
snaking through meadows
overflowing with glowing fat fishes
and buoyant green discs
as well as floating sewage,
the swollen dead,
rotting hulls of boats,
fish skeletons and traffic cones,
leeches, rats and cartoon boots.
The constant flow of light and night,
I am heavy with it.

This must be the river.
The one I've been waiting for
that carries me on
as everything does
but holds me as still
as anything moving could.

DISATTACH

You must have had some of
those phone calls
that make you put on your jeans at two a.m.
and drive to Dorset in the crying rain
to become a vessel for a person
who, when you leave,
will hand you bags of pain
for you to take back home and put away.

One day last year I crashed my car.
The policewoman said it was my fault;
the baggage in the back obscured my view.
She said she didn't want me to get crushed
under the weight of a car I had
no business driving at that hour.
Gripping polystyrene coffee,
I laughed because I don't want that either.

When you get those phone calls
you don't have to always drive there.
There's Uber, there's diazepam,
they'll probably be okay.

If you do decide to drive there,
put on your favourite jeans,
make a flask before you go
and sing to country music as you drive.
Not 'cause you're happy
but because you're well.
Relieved your face
is only wet with rain
and you're driving there,
but taking nothing home.

GOODBYE

I know I've been here too much.
Even in the ones about boats
I've been looming, haven't I?
Watching you thumb through
my joy and my mistakes.
No one likes to be watched eagerly,
unless it's by an audience or a large dog.

I tried to write myself out at times.
Thought about describing trees
but you know how to do that yourself;
it's called looking at a tree.
I didn't feel like trying to
make you see trees in a new light
when the old light's golden
and we're all so busy at the moment.

All I have are my mistakes.
I wanted to give them to you as a gift:
packaged with joy
and no return address.

ACKNOWLEDGEMENTS AND THANKS

'The Wrecking Season' and 'Rooftops' first appeared in *Under the Radar* in 2016 (Nine Arches Press).

'This Is the River' was commissioned by the BFI for *Britain on Film* in 2016.

'Earlham Cemetery November' first appeared in the *Bang Said the Gun* anthology in 2013 (Burning Eye).

Drive first appeared in the *North* (no. 48) in 2013.

'The Wrecking Season' is named after Jane Darke's film of the same name.

The Maureen Tucker quote at the front comes from an interview Maureen did with Daniel Coston in 1997. You can read the full interview at http://danielcoston.blogspot.co.uk/2013/10/moe-tucker-interview-1997-part-one.html

Cover design by George Payne.

I want to say thank you to these very important women: Lis Groenveld, Amy Nicholson, Megan Quinn, Chelsey Flood, Lisa Heledd-Jones and Danielle Brooke. I treasure your friendship, insight and comic timing. I would be a worse writer and person if I didn't know you.

Thanks also to Yanny Mac, Suz, Roo and the Big Dog Ferry. Home is where the river is.

9 781909 136878